50

Quotes and Affirmations to Help MAXIMIZE Your Life!

- By: Eric Foster II, M.S.

Dedication

I dedicate this book to the readers. To the individuals who've acquired this book in any fashion, I hope that this book serves you along your journey the way that its inception has served me along mine. I hope that this book eventually becomes an ever-present confidence builder, beginning weekly, daily, and even hourly. I hope that this book helps you define who you are, where you are, what you desire, and how you will achieve it. This book is intended to share daily deposits and investments that will truly maximize personal potential and lives through intentional actions.

In life, we are often encouraged to capitalize on our opportunities but not how to maximize them, resulting in a sense of contentment yet unfulfillment. What is the difference? Capitalizing on an opportunity is about "getting in where you fit in." Maximizing an opportunity is about propelling it to the next level. This differentiation is the same reason that first-class seats are more expensive than coach seats on an airplane. There is a drastic difference in the level of service and comfort. As you progress through this book, try to note takeaways from each lesson and start applying them to your life today! By the time you finish the book, not only will you have an understanding of the behaviors that have prevented you from maximizing your life, but you will also have a manual on how to correct them. This book is no magic formula to increase your net worth, but it is a guide to adding value to your life, occupation, and the people you impact.

Before you begin reading this gem, say these words out loud: "I am responsible for making my life the best experience I'll ever have!" Etch these words in your mind. Repeat them out loud anytime you feel distraught, helpless, or out of opportunities. Remember, you are responsible for making your life the best experience that you will ever have. You are the boss of your life! Hire, fire, promote, and demote people, jobs, and things as you deem necessary. See you at the top!

- Eric

Table of Contents

"Confidence is seeing yourself how the people that admire you do."

There is a glow in the eyes of those that love us. The dog that wags its tail when it knows its owner is home. The warm smile of a speechless baby as its mother comes to pick it up and hold it. That look that your lover gives you when they bask in a moment to appreciate your existence. These moments are all feelings of adoration. Confidence is the adoration of oneself and your abilities. Being overly confident can become problematic; however, the right amount of confidence invokes feelings of surety in who you are, what you're able to accomplish, and what you're deserving of. Adore yourself today. Be confident.

"Something positive is coming from your struggle."

Frederick Douglass once said: "If there is no struggle, there is no progress." He was an intelligent man that knew the power of affirmations, thoughts, and manifestation. Though Douglass lived in a time that none of us can recollect, his stance remains true. Places that require little to no struggle often come with little to no progress. The world does not give you what you desire unless you are willing to struggle and fight for it. It is important to note that while you labor, there is something positive at the end of your struggle. The future that you desire will manifest itself through the labor of your actions. Life uncertainties may impede your actions resulting in unexpected struggles. Remember, even your struggles put you one step closer to what you've been working for.

If you want to change your life, you must change your actions. During this change, you may experience difficulties, but perseverance will have its due.

"It's all about perspective;
you can either have the world in your hands
or the world on your shoulders."

To understand that perspective changes things is to understand one of the greatest forms of imagery and illusion. Have you ever walked by a piece of artwork and saw one image from one direction but as where you're standing changes, another image comes to life? The power of perspective has also long been used by the media to control the public. Understanding this power gives you the ability to control your own thoughts.

To "have the world on your shoulders" is an analogy used to create the imagery of holding an unbearable weight, something someone would want to avoid. Having the world in your hands is another analogy that paints the picture of one owning the world by holding it within their hands. Both analogies involve possessing the world, but, if you're so focused on carrying the world that you do not realize you possess the world, you may never see your position. Change your perspective.

To whom much is given, much is expected. The pressures of possessing the world, whether carrying or holding, are distinctive to you and only you. NBA star LeBron James has been scrutinized for a large part of his career. The mere thought of the pressure to perform well in major games would be overwhelming for some, making the idea of being an NBA star as much tantalizing as it is ___ dreadful. Yet, in taking things in stride, he's become a great husband, father, and the NBA's all-time leading scorer. Your daily problems, responsibilities, relationships, and job each present new opportunities for new perspectives. Take them in stride and change your perspective; it may change your life.

"The most important role you can play is your own. Don't stress yourself out trying to play everyone else's part."

Everyone loves a team player. It is a great quality to have because a great team player understands sacrifice. A team player also understands that there will be moments that may require taking a leadership role and putting their own desires to the side for the betterment of the team. Contrary to popular belief, in life, there are no team players. Every living person is responsible for their own success. Some people try to lessen that burden through life coaches, life partners, even business partners. The fact remains that you are ultimately responsible for your own decisions and actions. The most important part you can play is your own. That means that you cannot worry about the roles that others are playing in your life more than the role that you play in it. What role do you play? Victim? Coach? Starter? Injured? Back-up or fill-in?

Ultimately, it is important that you understand what it looks like to take accountability for your life. If your life was a Hollywood movie, you need to play the protagonist as if you're trying to win an Oscar award. Don't allow yourself to be outperformed by the co-stars in your movie. Take control of your life by taking accountability for your actions and decisions. For example, if you are sitting at a table and don't like what is being served, get up and find another table, or just go cook what you want on your own. It's up to you to create the best version of your life, and you do that by playing your role. No one else's role matters. Despite how the hurt and issues originated, you will have to work through the hurt that you've endured. With this book, the stage lights are on, the camera is rolling, and your audience awaits.

"Don't compromise your character."

Your character is the single most important thing that you have. Once it is questioned by someone, they will always remember that moment and question your intentions. For that reason, never compromise your character. When people see that your character will not be compromised, they trust you to be who you are. To have someone's trust may not seem like much of a benefit initially, however, to have someone's trust is a privilege. Trust is a gift that is only given once. An individual may repeat the act of giving trust but only if there was reciprocation the first-time trust was given. If the trust is broken, you may never see any part of it again. Goals work in a similar manner.

When you set a goal, you do it with intentionality. You make a goal that you believe is attainable over a specific amount of time. The person who sets this goal is typically someone who believes in your potential to reach them. This person could be yourself, a friend, or even a life coach. The point is when your goals are set, you have created a covenant between you and whomever it was that assisted in the deciding of these goals. In the process of trying to achieve these goals, your character may come under fire. You may find yourself questioning your dedication to these goals. The person that is questioning that dedication is no longer the same person that set them but the person who wakes up every day and holds themselves accountable to them. This is where character takes over.

If you can force yourself to be consistent and honor your covenant rather than listen to the excuses you have about why you should quit, you've maintained your character. This is how you build trusting relationships not only with yourself but also with others. At home, in the office, on the streets, in business deals, character is a requirement. Character is the universal key to many of the doors your future lies behind. In your refusal to compromise your character, you enhance trust within yourself and the trust others have in you.

"The longer it takes for you to move, the longer you will have to wait for results."

What are you waiting for? Every day that you've chosen to not work toward your goals is adding time to how long it will take for you to reach them. Explore what it is that is preventing you from starting. Is it that the goals that you have set are not truly what you desire? Are you afraid to fail? Do you not believe that your goals are attainable? If your answer is yes to any of these questions, then the solution is simple: SET NEW GOALS. Even the process of setting a goal is working towards a goal. Do what you must to find the answers to why you are pretentious to starting the work towards accomplishing your goals. Embody them and devour them. Once you've come to terms with what is prolonging your greatness, you can jump into action.

Imagine being Mark Zuckerberg's college roommate who decided to not co-found Facebook. He missed out on a multi-million-dollar opportunity because of his unreadiness. Think about Blockbuster refusing to do business with Netflix, ultimately resulting in the company filing for bankruptcy. The point is that people miss opportunities every day because they neglect to make moves that can positively impact their future.

What have you been considering that you believe could advance your career, finance, health, or even in your home life? Ask yourself, if you truly believe that whatever you may be considering could better you as a person, why are you hesitant to make the investment? As I wrote this book, I continued to put it off until I realized that this book was my opportunity to maximize my life. In finishing it, the feeling of accomplishment was far greater than the feeling of regret. Start today, start now, and get after it now.

"You're not waiting on the world;

the world is waiting on you."

It is important to note that your life will have an impact on the people with whom you interact based upon your gift. Dr. Martin Luther King, Jr.'s rhetorical skills unified people and allowed him to lead a revolution of freedom fighters until he was assassinated at age 39. Joan of Arc is remembered for her bravery and leading the French army to victory over the English in 1429. She died a martyr at age 19. Jesus Christ walked the Earth and made believers of millions through storytelling and working miracles until he was crucified at age 33. Dr. King, Joan of Arc, and Jesus all died before the age of 40. George Washington used his leadership to help found America, becoming president at age 57 and dying 10 years later. Colonel Sanders used his love for chicken to establish the Kentucky Fried Chicken restaurant chain in his 60's and lived to be 90 years old. My point is that each of these individuals possessed a gift that left an impact on the world. For some, this gift became prevalent early on in life while for others, it took shape during the middle to later years. You are not waiting on the world to recognize your gift; the world is waiting on you to properly present it.

On the journey to making your dreams become a reality or your passion your occupation, there will be a drawn-out period of, what may seem like, stagnation. This is not because the world doesn't appreciate your gift; the world is not ready for it. There are intricacies within you that you must first correct to maximize this craft. Usain Bolt was born to be the fastest man on Earth, but if he ran in the Olympics at ten years old, I am sure that we would be telling a different story. Similarly, you were born with a gift in you to impact the world and the people in it, but you must be fine-tuned to do this. Oftentimes, you hear stories of people quitting because they perceived that no one believed in them. They forgot that Rome was not built in one day. You can overcome this by remembering that the world is waiting for and needs your gift. You are not waiting on the world to recognize you. When you are primed for the recognition, it will come but you have to be prepared for it.

Wiz Khalifa is an artist that I watched developed. I remember Wiz releasing mixtapes and shooting music videos prior to signing a major record deal. His mixtapes were such a success that by the time he signed a major record deal and put out his first studio album in 2011, he was already primed for success. The album sold just shy of 200,000 copies in its first week and topped the US Billboard 200 at number 2! Shortly afterwards, I began to see Khalifa's influence through music. People everywhere were wearing Chuck Taylor shoes, camouflage shorts, and putting a blonde patch in their heads.

This was only the beginning of his success and influence, as he went on to release six more albums, star in movies, and perform at the Super bowl. Khalifa managed to attract all this success because he never quit. Even if a mixtape didn't attract the shows or money he desired, he kept making music. One day, he made the song that would launch his career and off it went. Had his fame come too soon, he may would have flopped, and never became the mogul that he is now. Only when his gift was primed was the world ready to accept it.

On your journey to maximizing your life, do not frustrate yourself wondering when your gift will give you the life you desire. Keep creating and crafting. This stagnant phase is increasing your potential energy, and when the time is right, it will turn into the kinetic energy that launches you into your desires.

"Let your work outweigh your words."

Affirmations and positive self-talk are great ways to get you going in the right direction of any goal, project, or desire. There is power in your words, and it should be utilized. There is more power in desire. Desire births your affirmations and positive words. Yet, unlike your spoken words, your desire should not end with the end of an affirming sentence. If your desire has not increased or been constant since speaking your affirmations, you will have a hard time transforming your words into actions. Your work must outweigh your words. The amount of work completed after your words have been spoken is what truly gives power to those words. Your desires being both empowering and influencing to your words should translate into measurable amounts of work and effort.

One of the most commonly used Bible verses I've heard is James 2:26, "for as the body without the spirit is dead, so faith without works is dead also." Speaking positive words is simply the beginning of action. The work that ensues is what makes those words come to life. If you falter in this transition from affirmation to implementation, then you can never reach confirmation. Preaching about your success won't be enough. You can sit in a car all day and say, "this car will start and take me to my destination", but until you physically start the vehicle, put it in drive, and use it for its intended purpose, the car will not be any good to you.

To maximize your life, take your desires and see them carried out until completion, your work must outweigh your words.

"Pace yourself."

Nipsey Hussle referred to life as a marathon, highlighting that it is continuous. Well, if life is a marathon, it is important that you pace yourself. Make time for the things that you enjoy. Who wants to reach their finish line only to realize that they never appreciated the race or the time it took to run it? In a race, the pace is more important than the distance. When you watch the Olympics, College, or High School track & field, or even a local 5k, each runner knows their pace. They have practiced their pace to know what a strong time interval looks like versus a weak one. Running too fast, too soon can bring fatigue in the final stages of your race. In contrast, a slow start can leave you with too much ground to cover and not enough time to cover it. Pace yourself.

To get the most out of life, you have to run your race at your pace. Everyone's journey to success will not be the same. Some people see success at an early age. Others may see their version of success come and go as it may not always not last long. Some may even have a steep climb up a rocky hill filled with setbacks and empty promises. This is still your race. Running, climbing, or even crawling at the pace that is best for you will make you the best version of yourself. You may have a ton of great ideas that you'd like to do in your lifetime, but you must remember that you have a__ lifetime to do them. Everything does not need to be done today. Pace yourself.

"Struggle, but don't quit."

It was already mentioned that there is no progress without struggle. For this exact reason, you cannot quit during the struggle. "Everybody has a plan until they get hit in the mouth" - Michael "Iron Mike" Tyson. Mike Tyson was arguably one of the most feared boxers of this time. A 5'10'', 220lb stick of dynamite! Mike was a lot shorter than most of his opponents, but Mike had the heart of a lion and feared no one. You must embody that same persona. Muster the heart of a lion. Be as courageous as Iron Mike when he stepped in the ring against an opponent.

Ask yourself, how many times have you drawn out a plan to accomplish a task only to reconsider following through because you faced some adversity? Think beyond the adversity and visualize who you would have been or what you could have accomplished had you stuck to your plan! The reason most people never get to maximize their life and reach their desired levels of success isn't because they're unlucky or because they're lazy, it's because of the burnout. After adversity hits, do you run out of gas, or do you push a little harder? When you get hit in the mouth, do you forget how much you sacrificed to get where you are, or do you weather the jab and keep fighting? To see things you've never seen, live a life you've never lived, or go places you've never been, you will have to struggle through adversity, but don't you dare quit.

"Being stagnant can block your blessings.

Sometimes you have to move so God can move."

Too often we wait for God to move when, in actuality, God is waiting for you to move. Your movement is a show of faith; it shows God that you are confident in what you want. That display of confidence gives God the opportunity to open all the doors and blessings reserved just for you. If you aren't sure of what you want, how can you expect God to give you anything? It's like walking into the food court in your local mall and seeing all these different options for eating. Behind every register is a group of employees waiting to serve you with a smile. You pass restaurant after restaurant trying to decide, and each time you pass, one of the employees smiles and are elated to greet you, but you just keep walking. When you finally find the place that you desire to eat, the employees can recognize your confidence and desire to order, and they open the opportunity for you to order from the menu. God works in the same way. God will hold your blessings until you've made clear what it is that you desire. Once you've begun to pursue whatever God has for you, God can begin to release what has been preserved for you.

Have you ever seen someone pursue something for far longer than they needed to, but for some reason they believed that it was for them? Things like promotions, relationships, skills, or careers, but __ once they shift their energy from what has consumed their focus, they fall right into their real purpose? It's no coincidence. When you start walking in your purpose, you will find that tasks become natural and enjoyable. Once you've reached this level, life begins to manifest itself. If you find yourself stagnant in your chase for what you desire in life, it may be time to explore other opportunities for movement.

"The moment you remove quitting as an option,

seeing yourself as victorious becomes easier."

Quitting, in some cases, may seem like the best option, especially when the odds are against you. When you're staring adversity in the face with sweaty palms and heavy breathing, you question your ability. What if I told you that you only doubt your ability because, in the back of your head, you know that you can still quit? That little scapegoat, no matter how small it is, is still big enough to influence you to abandon any progress, prior victories, or sacrifices that you have survived to get where you are. You have to dismiss quitting! Once you realize that quitting is out of the question, you naturally only see victory as an acceptable conclusion.

Imagine being on a roller coaster. Once that roller coaster starts, there is no stopping it. You've got one way to get off that ride, and that's by finishing it. It takes courage to pursue your goals, but it will take more courage to persist enroute to accomplishing them. When you begin to build a desire to quit, compare your journey to a roller coaster. They're fun yet intimidating. It feels like forever, but the ride is only a few minutes, and though you may panic, you're typically safe. The journey may intimidate you, but it will also enhance you. It may feel like it takes forever to complete your goal but it's only a fraction of your lifetime. Even when things seem to be going wrong, you are learning how to make them right. The only way to get off the ride is to finish it.

"The Bible says that you are salt and light

to the world. Don't let anyone

steal your flavor or dim your shine."

If the word of God has declared you as salt and light to the Earth, why would you let anyone dim your shine or steal your flavor? To be light is to illuminate dark places. You have this ability by being yourself. You're also so amazing that you add flavor wherever there is blandness. Everyone is not going to be accepting of your illumination nor your flavor. Some individuals like darker spaces, some like brighter spaces. Some individuals don't want too much flavor in their life because they like life to be repetitive. Other people love when life is full of flavor, and love seeing and doing new things daily. The bottom line is, don't stay in places where you are not accepted for being who you are. Always seek places where you are celebrated and not tolerated.

"The fear of failure is the love of comfort."

According to the Cleveland Clinic, fear of failure impacts 1 in 10 adults and 1-in- 5 teenagers. You can understand why when you factor in the fact that you have a great chance of failing at things you've never tried before. A lot of people quiver. The uncertainty in trying new things stems from the unfamiliarity of the unknown however, not all that is unknown or unfamiliar is bad. In fact, the unknown is enticing under the right circumstances. Think back to your child-like crush. You didn't know if they actually liked you but the rush that came with this uncertainty only enticed you further. Although you can see the twists and turns from afar, getting on a roller coaster for the first time still has some level of anxiety induced by uncertainty. Trying a new food as you enter adulthood comes with uncertainty, but the food is not always bad, right? This uncertainty brings us to a state of anxiety or arousal, spiking our senses and awareness for a brief period., Even so, we get on that roller coaster, we taste the foreign food, we even write that love letter to our crush. This quote reminds us to take that energy and channel it to conquer your fear of the unknown.

Some individuals would rather stay in a place of comfort out of uncertainty or fear of failing, even if it means living a subpar life. If you desire to maximize your life, then subpar living won't get it done. That means leaving these places of comfort, leaving fear and being willing to fail! Failing just means that you are trying. Failure means repetition. You have a 1000% better chance at becoming successful through failure than someone who fails to try because of their fear of failure. Consume yourself with your failures; this is where new knowledge and growth intersect. Genghis Khan, Napoleon, King Saul, King David were all leaders that acquired more than they were ever promised in life because they were not afraid to leave their comfort zone and challenge the fears that, subconsciously, directed them to stick with what they knew. I'm not encouraging you to go conquer a nation of people by force, but to channel that energy and conquer the day, the week, the month, the quarter, the year, and then, boom, your life!

"Vision is easy, action is a requirement,

and consistency is a necessity."

On any journey, from beginning to completion, you need at least three things: vision, action, and consistency.

Vision is the easiest of these to put into play. You can typically see vision in anyone. This is just being able to visualize something manifesting its way into existence. It requires nothing more than imagination and desire.

Action takes a bit more intentionality than visualization. With action comes consequences. Sometimes, this comes as victory, sometimes as defeat. More than likely, you will face both defeat and victory on a journey. Some things are going to work, but others won't. Between both victory and defeat, don't quit until you've accomplished the goal.

"With a task that's once begun, never leave until it's done. Be the labor great or small, do it well or not at all, always finish."

Consistency is the epitome of not quitting. Although it is its own pillar in the journey, it is highly relative to action. Consistency is the process of continuing your actions until you are successful, some may say relentlessly. The fact is that consistency is doing what's necessary, regardless of how you feel. When you wake up and don't feel like being consistent, combat that feeling with contentment.

When you feel yourself lacking motivation or wanting to quit, remember, vision is easy, action is a requirement, and consistency is a necessity.

"Control what you can control."

There are very few things that we can control at any moment in our life yet so many people get upset when things turn out differently from what they had hoped. If they understood that they can only control what they can control, they'd understand that, sometimes, probability is not in your favor. Effort and attitude are the only controllable features in life. When you change your attitude, you become open to different perspectives. When you change your effort, you afford yourself the opportunity to be the best version of yourself at any given moment. When you can combine the two, you are able to compete more effectively. Whether you're competing against someone, something, or yourself, you can compete more effectively. Think about sports when coaches see their players making mental mistakes based on emotion or feeling. They tell their players to get out of their heads. The same is true for everyday life. Get out of your head, give it all you've got, and compete.

"The room for improvement is the biggest room in the house."

We tend to forget that even in our greatest moments, there are still areas in our lives that can be developed and enhanced. The room for improvement is the biggest room in the house. This means that we can constantly evolve, grow, build, and add on to our lives. This room is never truly filled but consistently under construction. It is also important to note that this room reserves room for new ideas, passions, and opportunities. This room is conducive to all things that warrant the growth of the key holder. Use this room as you desire without inadvertently shrinking or downsizing it.

Improvement can sometimes carry a negative connotation. The need to improve on anything implies that you have not yet reached your best. Shift the paradigm of improvement to not being because of what you lack, but what you deserve, what your significant other deserves, what your kids deserve, and what the people around you deserve. Imagine if Henry Ford had never improved the Model T. Do you think Ford would have successfully sold that car almost a century later? The moral here is that anything that is not improving is losing.

There was a story on TikTok about Terry McLaurin, National Football League pass catcher. The story talks about how Terry attended an Ohio State University football camp and was told that he wasn't worthy to play at Ohio State. The head coach told him to go home and catch at least 200 passes every day then come back to show his improved ability to catch. Terry went home and did just that. He returned to Ohio State one week later and earned a scholarship after the coaches saw his improvement. He didn't shy away from his opportunity to get better because it would take intentional practice. Neither did he back down by saying that he would get an offer elsewhere. He gathered himself and began to craft and improve his game.

Sometimes, you may not have enough or be enough for what you desire. This does not mean you cannot become enough, but to become enough, you must be willing to improve on what you have. There is no reason to fear the room for improvement though, because it's the biggest room in the house.

"DO IT, but with shameless audacity."

"Only those who will risk going too far can possibly find out how far one can go." - T.S. Eliot. I could end this right here and enough would have been said, but there's a point to drive home. Shame is an emotion that defines deeply rooted embarrassment. It becomes prevalent when foundational human desires, such as the desire to feel safe and to belong, are not met. Creating such a strong overhaul of emotion, shame is something humans typically attempt to avoid. Audacity is defined as being imprudent, rude, or a willingness to take bold risks. Shameless audacity entails showing a lack of shame in these risks that may not sit well with everyone.

Success is a friend to no one. You will not see the best version of yourself by befriending every individual you meet or by not ruffling anyone's feathers. By no means does this mean put this book down and treat anyone inhumanely. However, everyone will not agree with the decisions you've made. This disagreement is not limited to coworkers or your opposers; it includes parents, siblings, spouses, and close friends. If you have concluded what is best for you, it is important that you display shameless audacity in your decision.

Family, friends, mentors, and even supervisors sometimes feel that they know what is best for us. While these individuals do provide great insight on some of our decisions, they could never know what is best for you. When I transferred from a community college to a university after not obtaining my associates degree, most of my family advised against it. They questioned a number of things: how would I make it at a university without being successful at a local college? Who would be my support system? What if I never finish and never get any degree? Despite the criticisms, I did as I pleased. I went on to earn a bachelors and master's degree from that university. Despite some of the people who had my best interests at heart being completely against my decision, shamelessly, I did what I deemed best for me.

Success may require drowning out the noise and focusing on your desired outcome, shamelessly. So what if you didn't get the results you desired in the first, second, or third year! Persistence is awarded when the time is right. Les Brown did a speech about how bamboo trees have to be watered every day for 5 years before the seed even breaks through the soil, but, once the tree breaks through the soil, it can reach its maturity within 5 weeks. So, start that business, start that fitness journey, start that new certificate or degree, or switch into that new career field. Just make sure you do it with shameless audacity.

"Change is inevitable; if you

don't create it, you must accept it."

For as long as the sun rises and sets, so shall the times of our lives. Today you can be the leader of a fortune 500 company and tomorrow, the janitor in the building across the street. Nothing will remain in place forever. Even our bodies, involuntarily, recycle our old cells for new cells from hours to years, depending on the cell's function. In life, change is going to happen if you are prepared or not. There is no saving us from the inevitable however, we can prepare for it.

If you are actively changing yourself to be in front of the prospective change that will come, you will fare better. Think of it as authoring your story instead of letting life author it for you. When you successfully do this, your evolution keeps you relevant amongst your bosses, employees, subscribers, or even your enemies. This relevance may pay off in recognition, bookings, raises, praise, or a reminder that you're still on your best game. If you neglect to initiate this change, you will quickly find your efforts becoming less and less recognized as if you've lost your common touch.

"Be who you say you are every day.

Consistency will follow."

Honesty is the best policy. So, why is it so hard for us to be honest with ourselves? Why do we believe lying is the best way to be the person we desire to see ourselves as? The journey of one million miles starts with a single step, but if we get up every day and tell ourselves we will take a step today but never do it, we're only extending that journey. Wake up and be exactly who you say you are every day. Each time you wake up, it may not be a day to take steps toward that million-mile journey; however, if you can discipline yourself to take those steps on the days you said you would, your habits and consistency will increase. Once it becomes a habit, you may find yourself doing a little more here and there: walking on days you didn't need to or taking extra steps on your walking days. Before you know it, that million-mile journey is done, and you've gained a new skill: consistency.

"Winning is a matter of execution; you either make excuses or you make a way."

The only place that success comes before work is in the dictionary. If you want to be successful in life, on your job, etc., execution is the key. Sadly, I can't tell you how much executing it may take for you to get your breakthrough, but no one can ignore elite execution. Terrell Davis is an NFL Hall of Fame running back. When he got his first opportunity to get in the game, he was a special teams player. One day his consistent effort paid off. He was routinely running down on kick coverage when he laid the ball carrier out flat! Coaches took notice of his consistent execution and decided to give him a shot as the starting running back. That shot produced a 7,607-yard and 60-touchdown career for Davis, all because of his ability to execute a completely different position from what he later became known for.

In your life, you must execute consistently, the same way Terrell Davis did on the field. This way when your moment comes you can crush it and make the most of your opportunity. No excuses are permissible. You must do the best with what you have until you can get better. Bloom where you've been planted and when it's time, you will get your shot to shine. If you want to win the day, the year, or even life, you must execute.

"Greatness is a bunch of small things done well."

Greatness doesn't start when you walk into your purpose. Greatness starts in your ability to do everything else. Simply put, greatness is a bunch of small things done well. The way you do anything is how you do everything. We like to confuse a great act as a once performed feat. The truth is that when somebody like LeBron James puts up jaw-dropping stats, or Elon Musk launches another rocket into orbit, we are not privy to the repetitions, actions, and work put in. It's these small things that both individuals do when no one is looking that gives them the opportunity to be great in public.

If you want to be great, you don't have to have everything together right now but at least start working on the pieces to the puzzle. Start mastering the puzzle and understanding all the moving pieces. Like a Rolls Royce, when all the pieces are being ordered to create the car, they are just pieces, but when the car is constructed, it's worth hundreds of thousands of dollars. You have to begin to understand the parts of your greatness and perform them well. Then, when your time comes, greatness will follow.

"Above all else, never fold."

This one is easy. Above all else, never fold. Many people have found themselves on the brink of their breakthrough, on the cusp of success, or on the eve of goal-actualization and they quit. Not that they knew how close they were to what they desired, but they let circumstance defeat them in their darkest hour. Now, as opposed to reaching their goals, they are left with the sour taste of dissatisfaction after hours, even years, of dedication to a goal, a mental chasm that they can not escape.

When you feel the desire to achieve anything threatened by unfavorable circumstances, think of the poem "Invictus" written by William Ernest Henley. In one of the stanzas he says, "under the bludgeoning of chance, my head is bloody, but unbowed." Meaning, though I have been beaten or abused by chance, though my luck has seemingly run out, I will not surrender or concede to the oppressor or circumstance.

The poem was written as Henley lay on his death bed mesmerized by the unknown and questioning which breath may be his last yet finding strength in being the master of his fate and the captain of his soul. When you begin to level with Henley's positionality in his poem, it is similar to desire. Desire is mortal and can have a length, like life. When you decide to give up or fold on your desires, they ___ begin to slowly die. If you can channel the same energy that Henley channeled in writing this poem, you too can be the master of your fate and the captain of your soul. This starts by deciding that even when the odds are unfavorable, you don't fold but instead, you stand tall on your desire.

"Sometimes, the difference between

acceptance and denial is tomorrow."

How long is too long? In the last chapter, we discussed why you should not quit on your goals. Now I ask you, how long are you willing to persist? If you are giving off the energy for what you desire for a year, what day do you give in and stop radiating that energy? Statistically, most people will ditch their new year resolutions within three weeks. That's 21 days, or 504 hours. That's not that long when we think about it. Think back to your childhood and how many times you asked your mother, father, grandparent, or whomever your caretaker was, for something relentlessly but the response was always no. Then, one day, you asked this same request, and the answer was yes! Do you remember the joy you felt? I'm sure you recall that serendipity far more than you recall how many times you made the request. Success works the same way. Sometimes, you have to ask again, in new ways, on different days, and even during different hours. What matters is that you request your desires repeatedly through your actions.

The truth is that you won't always get a "yes" the first time nor will you put out the energy to receive your desires or always be successful the first time you attempt to accomplish a goal. The race is not given to the swift, nor the strong, but to the one who endures. How long are you willing to endure? How many days will you wake up and get after your dreams, regardless of yesterday's outcomes? This is not the only way to make progress towards your goals, but you will find that most people who achieve greatness were entrenched in consistent progress rather than small spurts of success. Take some of your favorite musicians, for example. The most successful musicians and entertainers have made a supportive fan base by consistently releasing new projects as opposed to sporadically. In this sense, you have to also be consistent with your task, or what you put out when trying to accomplish a goal or obtain a desire.

"Even when you're down to nothing, your desires are greater than your obstacles."

How can I lose when I come here with nothing? A saying repeated countless times, it could even be considered as positive self-talk. Either way, sometimes being at the bottom of anything can be advantageous. When you know where your bottom is, then you no longer fear going there. When you've become accustomed to what your bottom looks like, you no longer fear starting from the bottom. So, even when you are down to absolutely nothing, anything given, received, or earned is more than what you have. For this reason, you have a lot more opportunities than obstacles.

To really understand this concept, ask yourself what your "bottom" is and what obstacles come with it? When people experience their version of the bottom, they try to get as comfortable as possible there, which you may have done. You may have even gone as far as setting minimal expectations to maintain this standard of your "bottom", and these expectations rarely come with any problematic issues as you want life to be as simple as possible. So, while you begin to set this new functioning bottom in your life, the sky is still the limit! In this case, your opportunities are far greater than your obstacles so, take advantage of them!

"Fatigue is a feeling, not an excuse."

Fatigue has plagued millions of people before. This feeling of being tired of doing anything is overwhelming. Sometimes, repetition comes with a lack of interest that impacts productivity negatively. In other instances, you may be physically drained and simply feel as though you cannot continue with a task. Well, fatigue is a feeling not an excuse. Our feelings will betray us, and even help us betray our goals. Being too tired to function is a great reason to rest but feeling tired because you want to do something different is not.

When you feel fatigue setting in, remember why you started and dig a bit deeper to pull out the best version of yourself. Muhammad Ali said that he never counts his reps when working out until they start to hurt because those are the reps that count. Becoming the best version of yourself is the same way. Doing the thing you normally do is always easy; they never present a challenge. When you start to feel resistance, that is when you know you have begun making strides. So, when fatigue kicks in, it is only telling you that you are now doing something you've never done. The biggest opportunity for growth comes from here and that is why it is important that when you hit that wall and begin to feel fatigued, you dig a little deeper. The resistance you feel is a natural reaction to you demanding what you desire instead of accepting what you've been given.

"It won't happen by chance. Get to work!"

Success is no roll of the dice, and even in the small chance that it is, it is typically after countless repetitions of trying other things. The best thing that you can do is start working. Things may not make sense at the beginning but through your work, you will make sense of it all. Luck is an imaginary thing that we have created to explain the feeling of obtaining something for which you did not work. Intention is everything, and no matter how small or big it is, it creates your luck. Therefore, you create your own luck, but the only way to do that is to begin working.

Luck only happens when Action Avenue meets Opportunity Street. Somewhere in that magical intersection, the intention and actions put towards a specified goal collide with a stage or platform to broadcast what you've been working on. For some people, this is an interview on the radio, a conversation with someone to whom they look up, or even an interview for your dream job. The fact is that you have to find your way to this intersection, and the only way to do that is by working to getting there. The man that you see on top of a mountain does not just fall there; there is more intention put into making it to the top of a mountain than that. It is in your best interest that you define your goals and start working towards them.

"Pressure bursts pipes

but it also creates diamonds."

In day-to-day life, too much pressure can cause someone to rupture or explode. Sometimes, we find ourselves under a lot of pressure and begin to hate where we are in life. But to be challenged is a privilege. To be called to greater purpose is a privilege that not all are afforded. Yes, pressure may burst pipes, but diamonds do not form without pressure.

When you begin to see this pressure as your call to greatness, you will then understand your privilege. That same heat and pressure that helps form diamonds is the same pressure that can turn you into a diamond. By no means does this mean put yourself under immense amounts of pressure to become a diamond version of yourself. However, when the pressure is acceptable and durable, stand strong! There is a fine line between too much pressure and just the right amount. When it's just the right amount, let it fuel you but if it is too much, I suggest finding healthy ways to alleviate some of that pressure.

"You have to want it more than the world

doesn't want you to have it."

Desire is defined as a strong feeling of wanting to have something, wishing for something to happen, or strongly wishing for a want. That is what you must have. The world is not designed or required to give you what you want simply because you want it. You must have a desire for your goals, a relentless desire. You will hear 'no' more times than you hear 'yes'. More people will prove to be roadblocks than bridges on your path to success. Therefore, desire is so important. There must be a will that is stronger than the resistance pushing against you.

When most individuals come face to face with resistance, they back down. In fact, courage can be defined as a resistance to fear. How many people do you know that truly exude courage? Imagine that those people are the only people who are willing to persist through resistance. Now imagine that this number of people is the only people you know to accomplish anything great. Would you be one of them? If not, it is time that you start working on becoming one of those people. Resistance represents the obstacles, people, and pitfalls that are going to come along your path to success. You must persist through them all. These pitfalls will naturally occur but how you respond will be the most important part of the outcome. When resistance hits, you have two choices: quit or persist. Most people __ will quit but if you want to see your optimal level of operation, you must be able to push through this. You have to want it more than the world doesn't want you to have it.

"Life is more than what we do. It is also

what we experience and who we become."

Life is about more than what we do. There is this odd belief that being busy means being productive. That notion could not be any further from the truth. Yes, production and accomplishments are important but so are your experiences. Life also consists of our experiences and makes us who we are. Your desires stem from what you have experienced. The reason that people usually want to be a doctor is because they had an experience that birthed that desire out of them. The same usually goes for athletes, preachers, teachers, and even pilots.

Sulk in your experiences to determine what it is that you truly desire in life. What moment was it that made you consider what you want most out of life? It is here that you will begin to find purpose in what you do. In finding your desire and purpose, you will begin to find value in what it is you do. When you reach this state, you begin to live life in its fullness.

"Things usually fall apart as other

things are falling together."

I have always been amazed by the recycling process. The fact that you can create something new with the pieces of something used is astounding. Think about how many items that you have used that are recycled and what it may have been in the former version of itself. Common household items that can be made from recyclable materials are toothbrushes, trash bags, furniture, and even clothes and shoes. All of these items may have had a completely different purpose before making its way into your life or home. Life can work the same way. A lot of people are creatures of habit and because of this, we like things to be the way they are. Sometimes, things stay the way they are for so long that we don't even know or remember its significance. Then, when things begin to unravel, we act like it's the end of the world because we don't know anything else. Some of the best things are discovered from the unraveling of others.

George Speck is the chef credited with the creation of the potato chip. As the story goes, Mr. Speck was cooking fries for a customer who had complained multiple times about their thickness. After the customer sent the fries back on multiple times, in frustration, Speck sliced the potatoes obnoxiously thin, fried them to a crisp, and coated them with salt. Believing the fries would be too thin, he awaited the customer's response only to find out that the customer loved what Speck had created. It was at this moment that the potato chip was born. Speck is now known as the inventor of the potato chip, however, during the circumstance of him believing he was ruining the fries he intended to make, he created something that would soon become just as popularized.

Think about where you are, where you've been, and how far you've come. Did things ever seem to fall apart so that other things could fall together? When your life began to fall apart, did you panic? Whether you panicked or not, did things eventually work themselves out? Keep these memories on your journey to maximizing your life! The journey may not be all smooth sailing, but smooth seas never made a skilled sailor. Sometimes, life is going to fall apart, dreams will fall apart, and action and execution may both fail you. Just remember, while it's falling apart, other things are falling together.

"Forgive if they did it on purpose. Forgive if they did it by accident. Bottom line: forgive

Free yourself from the emotion

attached to others' transgressions."

Forgiveness is not for the person who did you wrong, it is for you. You have to free yourself of the energy that you radiate when you think about what someone did to you. That energy is destructive and takes you away from abundance. When you think about what you missed out on because of someone else's actions, versus thinking in abundance, you take away from what you have attracted, and can continue to attract. Imagine you missing out on one thousand dollars because you keep recycling the energy of someone taking one hundred dollars from you. That is what happens when you concern yourself with past transgressions against you. Your mind becomes filled with disdain, regret, and possibly even envy. This distracts you from thinking in abundance and disrupts the flow of things being added to you.

When you forgive, you do not need to forget but you do need to make peace with yourself. Unfortunately, people will hurt you. Some intentionally, some unintentionally, but staying vexed too long serves you no purpose. It's better that you put the energy you would have used being upset into something constructive. Geno Smith is an NFL veteran quarterback. He had spent most of his career backing up starting quarterbacks regardless of a successful collegiate career. His pro career got off to a rough start as a part of the Jets organization. After parting ways with the Jets, Smith made a few more short-term stops at teams around the NFL finally landing in Seattle backing up superstar quarterback, Russel Wilson. He served as a backup to Wilson for three years before he got his opportunity to start. After resuscitating his NFL career, Smith put on the best performances of his entire professional career. When questioned, his response was, "They wrote me off, I ain't write back though." Meaning, he was doubted by many people, but he never subscribed to their doubting. He forgave his doubters but used their doubt as fuel to his fire. He completed the season as the starter and won the "Comeback Player of the Year" title. Soon after came the discussions of him potentially being one of the better free agents for the upcoming NFL off-season. Like Geno, use the feelings that you have towards your offenders as fuel to push yourself forward.

"Count the wins. Learn from the losses.

Put your heart in both."

In life, you will win. Make this affirmation this to yourself. In life, you will also lose. Accept this for yourself. No one ever shoots 100% or bats 1000%. In fact, LeBron James may very well finish his NBA career with the most points scored in NBA history by a single person, even if he has a 50% shooting average. Let's digest this. LeBron has been playing professional basketball since 2003. Over the span of his career, he has made half of the shots he's taken. Nevertheless, LeBron has been a world champion multiple times.

When you hear people speak of LeBron, they put his name in the company of the greatest basketball players from every era. Recently, he was inducted into the NBA's top 75 players to ever play the game, but still, he makes 50% of the shots he takes. That is what it means to count the wins. Conversely, LeBron shot 41% from the field in his rookie year. It was not until 2009 that he began to shoot 50% from the field. This is what it means to learn from your losses. Although LeBron was tagged to be one of the best to play the game since high school, eventually becoming the number one overall pick for the Cleveland Cavaliers in 2003, he worked on his game even after reaching the NBA. Learning from his losses, he took his shooting average from 41% to 50%. What does that look like? That looks like shooting the same shot in practice hundreds of times because you missed that shot in the game i.e., muscle repetition. That means building strength so that he could withstand contact when he goes for a layup in the paint. That also means training his mental and physical toughness to extend his stamina in both parts of his game.

Put your heart into both! When you see LeBron step on the court, it's the same pregame ritual. He pours powder in his hands and throws it up in the air letting you know that he's arrived. Some may say this is self-conceited, but when you work hard for something, naturally, you think highly of yourself. This is exactly who LeBron James is, a pillar of passion for the game of basketball. You can see the emotion in his face when calls don't go as he believed they should, or when he makes a momentous dunk or shot. You can tell he's putting all his heart into the game, win or lose. This is exactly how you have to be. As I stated, you WILL win in life. Affirm it. You will also lose sometimes so, accept it. Whether you win or lose should not impact how much heart and effort you put into winning. It's better to lose 100% of the time giving 100% of your heart than to lose once giving anything less. When you lose by giving 100% effort, you learn from that loss. But when you give 50% of your effort, it is a lot harder to improve because you did not use all your abilities in the first place.

So, win, lose, or draw, put your heart into every attempt at accomplishing your version of greatness!

"You won't spend a lifetime in this season,

but you will spend a lifetime with its reason."

Just as seasons and weather change from day to day, so will the seasons in your life. Some seasons will be like spring on a remote beach, enjoying your favorite beverage, book, or stick (for the cigar smokers). Others will remind you of an uncompromising, arctic winter breeze. For some reason, those harsh seasons seem to teach us a lot more than the seasons that we find enjoyable however, there are lessons in both. If you find yourself too busy enjoying the shade and sun in the spring, you may miss the lesson. However, when we feel the arctic blast of a freezing gust of wind, we automatically clench our coats to cover up as much as possible to avoid the cold, learning our lesson expeditiously, in most cases.

The best part about seasons is that they change so, come winter, spring, fall, or summer, be prepared for things to change but don't forget the lessons. A wise individual does not become wise to anything without having first lived it. A season of greatness or season of turmoil, both will bring new knowledge. Your application of this knowledge may easily extend or shorten your season. If the secret to becoming a millionaire within one year was told to two average-earning individuals but only one of them applies the knowledge, you may very well see their season change in the form of early retirement, net worth, and quality of life. The individual who neglected to apply any of the secrets may remain in the same season of life working an average paying job. Even if this individual starts 30 days later than the now millionaire co-worker, they have extended that season of their life working an average paying job. What happens if they take the information and work twice as hard, turning that year into six-months? They then immediately shorten that season and may be a millionaire at the end of the six-months.

Wisdom comes from understanding what surrounds you. As you move through the different seasons of life, try to find the lessons in each sunny day and each chilly night. The seasons won't last but the lessons will.

"There are 86,400 seconds in one day.

All you need is one to be great."

There are so many moments throughout one day. We only need one of these to be great. All it takes is one second out of your day to do something great that could change your day, week, year, or life. The second Curtis "50 cent" Jackson decided to use the term "get the strap" and trademark it, it later made him one million dollars. The term was not new to those who had been using it for years, but when Jackson started using it, he became one million dollars richer. The same is true for anyone who has seen high levels of success. There was one point in their careers that something just clicked that launched them into their success story. Yes, the shift happens over a period but that may be before, after, or even in-between the second that you became great.

When a basketball game comes down to the last shot, everyone remembers the game, but the greatest highlight was the second the final shot went in. For this exact reason, Michael Jordan's retro 14 black and varsity red colorway was labeled the "last shot 14's," because they serve as a replica of the shoes that Jordan hit the championship winning shot to end regulation in the 1998 NBA finals versus the Utah Jazz. The point is that of the 86,400 seconds in one day, it only takes one to be great. It only takes one second out of the day to change your entire life, for the rest of your life.

"You will be separated by what becomes of your

work ethic, not by what comes out of your mouth."

Have you heard the saying, "I'd rather see a sermon than hear one?" This saying simply means to show me, don't tell me. Success is not a gimmick around which you can build up hype and expect situations to change based on the enticing smoke screen you've portrayed for the naked eye. You see, even ignorance becomes wise over time, and no matter how you dress it up, a pig will still live like a pig. Your work ethic separates you and not what comes from your mouth. Anyone can talk a good game about who they are, some are even crazy enough to believe themselves. Fewer can execute the actions of which they speak.

The growth and experience are not in how well you can dictate what you want to do, but how faithful to the journey of becoming the person you speak of becoming. The manifestations and quotes in this book are evidence enough. You may pick this book up, read a quote, and be empowered, but how are you turning the potential energy into kinetic energy? Yes, you've been charged up but what you do after you close this book is what will separate you from everyone else. Do more than that of which you speak.

The Grand Canyon was created by a quiet river. What seemed like peaceful, flowing waters, were eroding the rocks around it all along until it created what we now know as the Grand Canyon! Success works the same way. Keep working in silence, and like the Colorado river creating the separation between the sides of the Grand Canyon, you'll create separation between yourself and those who desire to have what you've worked for.

"Don't be afraid to be the only person

that believes in you."

If you are waiting for the support, you may be waiting forever. No one is going to save you but yourself. You may have to start the journey without support, and that is ok. Stand for what you believe in. In the movie Forrest Gump, Tom Hanks plays a character that exceeds expectations in all parts of his life. There is one scene that comes to mind. There came a time in the movie where Forrest got up off the porch and just started running. He ran one step at a time, across the country with no intention of doing so when he started. Forrest ran for over 3 years and started garnering national attention, ending up on TV. As he ran, reporters ran with him asking why he was running, the purpose of doing this for so long, and the philanthropy that ignited his run. Forrest said, "I just felt like running" and sped off. With the buzz from his running, people began to follow him slowly but surely. It started with one person but by the time he decided he had run enough, he had a small cult of runners following him.

Forrest never asked anyone to join him; he just knew what he needed for himself. He believed in himself enough to just run and as simple as it sounds, that is what made people believe in him. As you start your run, don't be afraid to be the only person believing in you. Followers will show up naturally when it is time, but in the infancy of your journey, just know that you may be the only one who

believes. Keep believing.

"Build strength in your weakest moments."

One of my coaches used to always say, you are only as strong as your weakest link. Greek mythology talked about the warrior Achilles being feared by all his enemies. While he was immortal, there was one thing that could kill him: his feet, which were his weakness. Shaquille O'Neal is arguably one of the greatest centers to ever play basketball, but his free-throws were his weakness. Needless to say, everyone has a weakness and if you are only as strong as your weakest link, it is important that you build strength where you are weak.

Most people want to improve their strengths because it makes them feel empowered. Shaq was great at rebounding and put-back dunks, but everyone remembers him for his inability to shoot free throws. Achilles's foot weakness story has grown so popular that the saying, "Achilles heel", was developed referring to his weakness. To say the least, you will be remembered for your weakness when you are not working to make your weakness a strength. To combat this, build strength in your weakest moments. When you are down to seemingly nothing, that is when you fight the hardest. Not because you want to but because you want to hold on to the little bit of what you have left. That's a natural response. When does a dog become most defensive? When it understands that it is fighting for survival.

Survival may entail fighting for a place to sleep, something to eat, or general health and welfare. People work the same way. In most cases, when we are weak, we may become defensive. There is nothing wrong with this but make sure you are building strength during this time.

Take what has historically defined you as weak and make it into a strength. When you find yourself in one of your weaker moments, you can rest assured that though it is not your strong suit, you have built some resilience to withstand discomfort or tests. The hope being that the resilience you've gained where you were once weak, will carry you through these unbearable moments in the future.

"Opportunities that don't align with your goals are distractions."

Distractions are defined as things that prevent someone from giving their full attention to something else, a diversion or recreation, or an extreme agitation of their mind or emotions. However you define it, know that they are not needed as a part of our journey.

It has been said before, the quickest way from point A to point B is a straight line. Distractions can make a straight line look a lot like the crooked letters that come after M and I in the word Mississippi. In a lot of these cases, the distraction comes looking like the opposite of what it actually is. Distractions typically look like shortcuts, better opportunities, vices, and sometimes relationships. This is not to say that you should not maintain relationships, or you cannot enjoy yourself on a well-deserved night after you've worked intentionally over time. However, like everything else in life, too much of anything is a bad thing. Even a glass of wine is heart conscious in moderation. The problem begins when these distractions become a hindrance to your progress.

Who are you when it's time to get rid of your distractions? Are you able to turn away from your distractions for a period to help you double up on a goal? That will tell you how much of a distraction something can be to you. To be successful, you must have sober judgment, methodical precision, and true devotion. That means your heart should not be condemned with anything outside of the necessities which could include family, close friends, and desire.

You must learn to differentiate between these distractions and opportunities as they will cause you to focus your intentions elsewhere for long periods of time and lose track of what it is that you truly desire. Remember the goals you have set for yourself and design what the path to accomplishing them may look like. This will help you identify when newly presented opportunities will empower or distract you from your focus.

"Recognize what you've outgrown and

leave it where you left it."

Holding on to things can help you understand that all good things come to an end. However, holding on too long can leave you frozen in a place of sadness and stunt your growth. You have to recognize the things that you have outgrown, and then leave them where you left them.

Growth is important in any journey. Being able to identify that you've outgrown old habits is key! You cannot make it to your destination if you cannot get over leaving your current station. The people who have these rags to riches and success stories that we hear about all have something in common: they understood when it was time to move on from relationships, friendships, jobs, and careers. You may love that person, place, or thing but it may not be able to go where your next level of growth is taking you. You have to leave that connection where you left it so that you can form new connections, better and more essential connections. You can always appreciate what was, but you cannot let what should have been a moment turn into an eternity.

Holding on too long is the downfall of many people. It keeps your hands full of unnecessary items or relationships making it impossible to catch the next opportunity in front of you. Imagine if Oprah was so tied up in coping with losing her first job that she was not open to new opportunities. Imagine if Mac never rebranded as Apple and produced the iPhone because their hands were tied up appreciating their past. Neither Oprah nor Apple would have been prepared to receive the new opportunities in front of them. Recognize what you've outgrown and leave it where you left it so that your growth can continue

"People and feelings are temporary so,

do what's best for you."

Feelings come and go, and for that reason, they should not control your actions, responses, or decision making. You may not feel like today is the day to do the task that you have been telling yourself you would do for two weeks, but when you made that promise to yourself, you made a covenant with yourself. Why would you let something as temporary as your feelings force you to break a promise that you made to yourself? You may not feel like completing that task today, tomorrow, or the next day but you have to do what is best for you. That goes for your friends, spouse, family, and your feelings. You have to do what is best for you to become the best version of yourself. People will adjust to your decisions and journey. Your goals are unforgiving and don't adjust. They don't come at discounted rates.

Do you remember the times as a child that something would happen, and it seemed like your life was turned upside down? Maybe it was someone stealing your bike, your crush turning you down, or you found yourself throwing a fit for not getting permission to sleep over at your friend's house. Whenever events like this happened, you may have thought that you would never recover from the tragedy and that life as you knew it may fail to exist beyond that point. Years later, look at you reading this book to enhance your life and working towards accomplishing new goals, hardly, if at all, affected by those traumas!

Your willingness to proceed through life and become greater despite those events, is what has gotten you to this point. Your ability to continue striving for greater is what will get you to the next. So, when you find yourself upset or unmotivated, remember that this too shall pass and after it passes, you will be better or worse based on your ability to persevere, despite your feelings.

"There is no such time as the right time."

It does not matter how many times you read a clock; you will never read the word "right" on it. The reason why is because there is no such thing as the right time. We've been conditioned to believe that we should be waiting on variables outside of our own intuition when it comes to our accomplishments. If you wait on another person, your aspirations could expire while waiting for your version of the perfect opportunity. Meek Mill said it best, "chances are never given, they're taken like interceptions." You waiting for your chance, turn, or the right time may have you waiting 10 years for an opportunity that you could have given yourself in six months. Stop waiting for the right time. Get After It Now.

"Escape your excuses."

Accomplishing goals requires a third "E.Y.E." vision. In this case, E.Y.E. stands for Escaping Your Excuses. You may have made some promises to yourself this year in the form of goals. Deciding what you desire is the easy part. The hard part is consistency. Waking up every day at 6 am to do yoga, attending your religious group's convening every week, and being on time for important events are all great goals for the year. However, after you set these goals, executing them every day gets hard.

Some days, you are going to wake up and not want to do what you promised to yourself. When these days come, ask yourself, is this an excuse? Things naturally happen in life that throw us off our schedule, which is ok. What is not ok is throwing ourselves off our schedule because of excuses. An excuse is, "I don't feel like it", "I made other plans", or "I'll go tomorrow." These are a few of the top excuses we use for things that we do not want to do. To tell the truth, you may have more days where these excuses play in your head than days that they don't. Starting a new journey is always exciting until you realize how far you must travel. For these reasons, you must learn to escape your excuses to reach the destination or goal that you desire.

"Failure initially sounds bad, but failure is

the best teacher for future behavior."

The best determinant of future behavior is past behavior. In failure, we lose but we learn. Understanding that what has failed us once, will more than likely fail us twice. What has failed before will most likely fail again. When we come to understand this, we begin to understand ourselves. When you know what actions and habits have caused you to fail, you then know what not to do if you desire to win. The lessons that come from failure will teach you far greater lessons than your successes. The reason your elders are so wise is rooted in their experience. When you've seen or experienced something, prior knowledge gives you an upper hand in competition. Your favorite superheroes and villains are archnemesis because they've studied each other so well that they can almost guess each other's moves in combat. This is why we should look at failure as an opportunity to get better rather than an embarrassment to ourselves.

Fail your way to the top. It sounds ignorant but it's the best mindset to have! Do you remember learning how to count to 100? When you first started, getting to 10 was a task. Once you could count to ten, you may have fumbled your way to 20 a few days later, then somehow 50, and so on until you reached 100. You tried every day until failure but eventually, failure was no longer an option. It's the same psychology behind learning to ride a bike. You start off with training wheels, then just two-wheels and usually you fall a few times before becoming good at it.

Whether it was falling off that bike or fumbling your numbers to 100, all are progressive movements on the road to success. It's better that you fail and learn than to not try at all and become stagnant. So, try that new activity. Try that new meal plan. Try that new daily routine. It is through our trying that we get better.

"You're only as successful as your energy

warrants. You'll never get out more

than what you put in."

As people, we understand that for every action, there is a reaction, That's Newton's third law. Yet for some reason, we don't believe this applies to us being successful. There is a sense of entitlement to being successful. People believe that because they've done what they consider to be enough, they should see results. Being successful or completing a goal is just not that simple.

The tree does not bear fruit the first day you plant the seed. The tree will not bear fruit the first week, month, or year. In fact, it takes an average of three to four years for a tree to bear fruit. In the process of getting this tree to bear fruit, there is a lot of nurturing, pruning, and even propping up the tree. All these things take energy and, believe it or not, still does not guarantee that the tree will bear fruit or that it will bear the amount of fruit you've envisioned. There are no cheat codes for hard work. There are, however, spoils for it. Hard work is rewarded in breakthroughs. Sometimes, these breakthroughs are visible, sometimes they are not. However, your breakthrough will never come if you are not putting the work in. If you are not expanding your energy, there will never be a return of energy. Even when you expend your energy, the chances are slim that the reciprocation of that energy will be equal to, or greater than, the energy that you've burnt.

Every sport has a championship game. Each game has two teams competing for distinct rights to that championship. The players on each team lace up and give their best effort to win the game however, there can only be one winner. All these players give their best effort, but all of them cannot claim to be a champion at the end of this game. Success is similar. You give your best effort and do not always get the results you desire, but you will never get out more than you put in. So, if you have any intention of achieving what you desire, do more than what is required.

"You trust everyone else but

why do you doubt yourself?"

Think about all your beliefs. Most people believe in a group of things outside of their control, For example, you believe in your religion, and some even believe it enough to be a martyr for it. You believe in your job, otherwise you probably wouldn't show up every day and would be looking to work elsewhere. You believe in your education, understanding that you've learned the necessary skills to work in a field or trade upon completing your education. You believe that your alarm clock will wake you up no matter what time you go to sleep. Lastly, some people believe in their car to start up every day and transport them from point A to point B. The question is, why do you believe in so many things around you, but you refuse to believe in yourself?

Sometimes, alarm clocks fail. Sometimes, jobs ask you to do things that go against your morals. Sometimes, your car won't start. Yet we put our faith in them every day to work the way we need them to work. By no means am I saying, lose faith in your car, religion, job, or education, but I am asking you to give yourself the same grace that you give to these things so that you can begin to believe in yourself.

When someone's car won't start, what do people do? They talk nicely to the car as if the car is listening. This is practicing both ___ positive self-talk and manifestation. When people come across something in their religion that they don't agree with, what do most people do? They take it with a grain of salt but retain their belief in their religion. How about when your boss is coming down on you and you think that you have done the best that you can do? You find a way to improve so that your boss doesn't come down on you like that again. My point is, if you can believe in all these things, why not believe in yourself?

"Your faith is bigger than your problems."

"You of little faith," four words Jesus Christ said before calming the storm to save his disciples. The disciples were sure that had they not gone to Christ, they would have died. They did not realize that they possessed the strength to calm the storm the whole time, strength known as faith. They did not know how to use it yet. The Bible says that if you have the faith of a mustard seed, you can tell a sycamore tree to move and so it shall move. Just as the disciples possessed the power to conquer the storm, you have the power to conquer your storm, but you must activate it. Let your faith be bigger than your problems. Too many times people have faith in something for weeks, months, and years and then allow a problem to shake their faith. If you have faith, half of your problem is already solved. You may not know the how, but faith is your why.

"Your preparation will make your

"moment" that much sweeter."

Have you ever waited on something and when it came, it was a moment you could never forget? Imagine your grandmother preparing Thanksgiving dinner the night before the feast. Close your eyes and imagine the aroma of pies, cakes, sides, and turkey filling the house from the moment you go to sleep until the moment you wake up, but the preparation continues. Well into Thanksgiving Day, she's still cooking as your mouth salivates thinking about the moment you get to sit down in front of your prepared plate. Then, everyone gets together to bless the food and the feeling intensifies. You're only minutes away from what has taken all day and night to prepare, and then boom! You bite into a meal that you'll reminisce about well into the new year.

My point is that the entire time the meal was being prepared, you knew it would be good, but you knew it would take time as well. When you finally got your opportunity to eat, you were probably overcome by a feeling of satisfaction as you indulged in your favorite foods. Success is no different. The preparation makes the moment sweeter. The time you spend preparing for your opportunity will amplify the glory of your breakthrough moment. Do not be discouraged or dismayed when things don't happen on your time. Instead, remind yourself that it is the preparation that makes the ___ moment. Do not be discouraged or dismayed when things don't happen on your time. Instead, remind yourself that it the preparation that makes the moment.

"Win, lose, or draw, you will be better

today than you were yesterday."

Rick Ross said, "Every day that you wake up, you're richer than you have ever been." Break that down. How could a person sleeping on the street be richer than he's ever been by waking up? What about the CEO who lost millions the night before, how is it that he can wake up in a deficit compared to his previous wealth and be richer than he's ever been? Riches are measured in more than the accumulation of currency. Every day you wake up a little bit wiser. You wake up with or to new knowledge, which is also wealth. When you wake up to new knowledge, you can get better at something. Better at how you chase your dreams, and it's these opportunities that make you richer than you've ever been.

The knowledge that you gained the day before, put it to use. Win, lose, or draw, you gained new knowledge that you can test out tomorrow. As long as you're trying, you can't lose; it's a steppingstone in the process to becoming the best version of yourself.

A millionaire is not a millionaire because he is worth a million dollars. It is the wealth of knowledge on how to make a million dollars that makes a millionaire a millionaire. So, after every day, win, lose, or draw, you become better and richer than you've ever been.

"Life is an occasion; rise to it!"

Have you ever been in a room where everyone is seated comfortably until someone important walks in? You then see everyone stand-up to give respect to the individual that is walking in. Or you may have heard someone say rise or stand for the occasion. Well, life is an occasion. We are here for a few short decades and then we are gone forever. Why are we so intrigued by standing for an occasion but living life as though we have all the time in the world? I have often heard people say that the graveyard is the wealthiest place because it is often filled with dreams unrealized, and goals left unaccomplished. Life is an occasion, and you must rise to it to live out your true purpose, or you risk experiencing life as a fraction of the individual you could have been.

Notes

Notes

About the Author

Eric Foster is a higher education practitioner from Port Salerno, Florida. As a result of his mother's strong faith and keeping Eric and his siblings in church as frequently as possible, Eric

mirrored that same faith and now sounds pastor-like when he speaks. Though his faith is a major component of his foundation, Eric would be the first to tell you that he's not a pastor, he's a survivor. Eric's world was turned upside down when he lost his mother at age 11. He was a problematic child before her passing, but he would only become harder to deal with as his siblings took on the role of primary caretakers. In his formative teenage years, Eric found himself spending more time kicked out of school or serving in-school suspensions than in class. During this time, Eric admittedly saw little, if any, promise for his future and praised worldly possessions. When Eric turned 20 years old, he decided that he wanted better for himself. Eric then re-enrolled at Valencia College in Orlando, Florida, earning enough credits to transfer to Florida International University (FIU). Over the coming years at FIU, Eric would earn a bachelor's and master's degree in education and sports management, respectively. Currently, Eric is a doctoral student at Florida Atlantic University pursuing a Ph.D. in higher education leadership. His educational and research focus are Black male experiences in post-secondary education and their graduation and retention rates. In his time away from school, Eric uses his adverse experience as a child to inspire, empower, and motivate others to their own version of greatness.

Made in United States
Troutdale, OR
08/03/2023

11787889R00086